SLAVERY
IN AMERICA

RECONSTRUCTING THE SOUTH

By Duchess Harris, JD, PhD

with Nel Yomtov

Essential Library

An Imprint of Abdo Publishing | abdobooks.com

Published by Abdo Publishing, a division of ABDO, PO Box 398166, Minneapolis, Minnesota 55439. Copyright © 2020 by Abdo Consulting Group, Inc. International copyrights reserved in all countries. No part of this book may be reproduced in any form without written permission from the publisher. Essential Library™ is a trademark and logo of Abdo Publishing.

Printed in the United States of America, North Mankato, Minnesota.
032019
092019

Cover Photo: MPI/Archive Photos/Getty Images
Interior Photos: JimEngelbrecht/Danita Delimont/Alamy, 4–5; Red Line Editorial, 9, 14; iStockphoto, 10; Everett Historical/Shutterstock Images, 12–13, 19, 22–23, 29, 49, 51, 57, 63, 67, 74–75; Rogelio V. Solis/AP Images, 17; World History Archive/Newscom, 27; Everett Collection/Newscom, 34–35, 43; Picture History/Newscom, 37; Pictorial Press Ltd/Alamy, 39, 82; North Wind Picture Archive, 46–47; Archive Photos/Getty Images, 60–61; AP Images, 73; Johanna Huckeba/AP Images, 79; Stocktrek Images, Inc./Alamy, 84–85; American Photo Archive/Alamy, 89; Monkey Business Images/Shutterstock Images, 93; Michael Brochstein/Sipa USA/AP Images, 96

Editor: Alyssa Krekelberg
Series Designer: Laura Graphenteen

LIBRARY OF CONGRESS CONTROL NUMBER: 2018966008

PUBLISHER'S CATALOGING-IN-PUBLICATION DATA

Names: Harris, Duchess, author | Yomtov, Nel, author.
Title: Reconstructing the south / by Duchess Harris and Nel Yomtov
Description: Minneapolis, Minnesota: Abdo Publishing, 2020 | Series: Slavery in America | Includes online resources and index.
Identifiers: ISBN 9781532119262 (lib. bdg.) | ISBN 9781532173448 (ebook)
Subjects: LCSH: Slavery--United States--History--Juvenile literature. | Reconstruction (U.S. history, 1865-1877)--Juvenile literature. | Emancipation of slaves--Juvenile literature. | African Americans--Civil rights--Juvenile literature. | Racism--United States--History--19th century--Juvenile literature.
Classification: DDC 326.9--dc23

CONTENTS

CHAPTER ONE

An Unprecedented Challenge

On the chilly evening of Thursday, January 12, 1865, a group of African American leaders of the black community in Savannah, Georgia, met with US secretary of war Edwin M. Stanton and General William Sherman. The meeting was held at the Green-Meldrim House in Savannah. The house had been the general's headquarters since Union forces had captured the city several weeks earlier. The Civil War (1861–1865) was nearing its end.

Many of the black attendees were ministers in the Baptist and Methodist churches of Savannah. The men included formerly enslaved people. At the time, William Bentley was 72 years old. He had

Today, people can tour the Green-Meldrim House.

been a slave until the age of 25. Former slave John Cox, age 58, had bought his freedom in 1849. And 72-year-old Glasgon Taylor had been a slave until he was freed by the Union army.

The leader of the group was Garrison Frazier. He was born into slavery in Granville County, North Carolina, in 1798. Frazier remained enslaved until 1857, when he paid for his freedom for himself and his wife in gold and silver.

The meeting was Stanton's idea. He hoped to create a plan to provide housing, food, and employment for the thousands of enslaved people who had left plantations in the region and followed Sherman's army to Savannah. They discussed the future for freedmen.

When Frazier was asked whether he would prefer to live scattered among the whites or in a black colony, he said, "I would prefer to live by ourselves, for there is a prejudice against us in the South that will take years to get over; but I do not know that I can answer for

SLAVERY: MOTIVATION FOR SECESSION AND WAR

While slavery was not the only cause of the Civil War, the writings of Confederate leaders indicate that slavery played a central role in states' secession from the country and the war that followed. On December 20, 1860, South Carolina became the first state to secede from the Union. In its declaration of secession, delegates from the state affirmed that President Abraham Lincoln's election in 1860 as "President of the United States, whose opinions and purposes are hostile to slavery" was motivation for secession. In no uncertain terms, the delegation proclaimed "that a war [would] be waged against slavery until it shall cease throughout the United States."[1] The Mississippi declaration of secession stated, "Our position is thoroughly identified with the institution of slavery."[2]

Alexander Hamilton Stephens of Georgia, a member of the US House of Representatives, wrote in 1850 that "the great question of the permanence of slavery in the Southern States" was all-important for preserving the Union.[3] Later, as vice president of the Confederacy, Stephens proclaimed that slavery provided the basis of the new government: "Its foundations are laid, its corner-stone rests, upon the great truth that the negro is not equal to the white man."[4]

my brethren.”[5] Frazier also noted that the best way for freedmen to take care of themselves was to have land.

After a brief discussion of Savannah's occupation by Union troops, Stanton ended the meeting. The black leaders had expressed their goals as emancipated people. But they knew free African Americans faced an uncertain future—one that ultimately delivered significant triumphs, grave disappointment, and even bitter hostility and violence.

THE END OF WAR, THE END OF SLAVERY

On April 9, 1865, Confederate general Robert E. Lee surrendered his troops to Union general Ulysses S. Grant. The Civil War was over. But the Union's preservation came at a shockingly high cost. Roughly 620,000 Americans died in the fighting and 476,000 were wounded. An additional 400,000 people had been captured by either Union or Confederate forces or were missing.[6]

Among the most critical consequences of the war was the end of slavery in the United States. The first enslaved Africans came to the American colonies in the early 1600s. This human bondage existed throughout the country, though by the start of the 1800s, Northern states began to emancipate enslaved people.

Slavery boomed in the South, where labor was required to farm cotton, tobacco, and other crops. At the start

WHITE INCOME AND SLAVERY[8]

	Percentage of Population That Was Enslaved	Percentage of White People's Income from Slavery
Alabama	45	41.7
Arkansas	26	17.4
Florida	44	33.6
Georgia	44	29.4
Louisiana	47	23.6
Mississippi	55	29.2
North Carolina	33	19.4
South Carolina	57	35.8
Tennessee	25	18.3
Texas	30	19.4
Virginia	32	17.4

Slave labor was the basis of the South's economic prosperity. Any action by the US federal government to limit or abolish slavery posed a significant threat to all white Southerners.

of the Civil War, around four million slaves lived in the United States. Three million slaves lived in the 11 states that seceded from the Union to form the Confederate States of America in 1861: Alabama, Arkansas, Florida, Georgia, Louisiana, Mississippi, North Carolina, South Carolina, Tennessee, Texas, and Virginia.[7] Slavery was the backbone of the Southern agricultural economy.

Enslaved people working on a plantation field often toiled for many hours in the hot sun.

ENSLAVEMENT AND FREEDOM

Southern states maintained an ever-tightening grip on their economic lifeblood. Slaves were property with no legal rights, and they lacked citizenship. No slave could own guns, testify in court against a white person, or leave a plantation without permission. Enslaved people were often separated from friends and family. Brutal beatings and whippings were commonplace. The entire slaveholding system "was committed to enforcing the masters' control over their human property," according to historian Eric Foner.[9]

With the Northern victory in the Civil War came the abolishment of slavery, and questions arose. People wondered what freedom truly meant. They also questioned whether freed slaves should have the same rights, such as the right to vote, as white men. People also waited to see how the South would respond to such revolutionary change. Would Southerners accept the social, political, and economic changes emancipation was certain to bring? In addition, people wondered who would create and oversee the plan to incorporate the former slaves into US society.

The years 1865 to 1877 are generally considered the era of Reconstruction. This was a time during which the issues of emancipation and readmitting the seceded Southern states back into the Union were addressed. The victorious North and the defeated South faced a challenge unprecedented in US history. The decisions made during this critical era would have dramatic effects on African American life not just in the late 1800s but also for many decades to come.

CHAPTER TWO

THE STATE OF A NATION

The Civil War reshaped the United States. Social, economic, and ideological changes in the North and South required policy makers and citizens to reunite and rebuild the divided nation. Although the war was over, the Confederate states still had to rejoin the Union. The economy of the South was devastated. How would Americans confront the legacies of their long, bloody war, and what would be the consequences of their actions?

COUNTRYSIDE IN RUINS

One major visible impact of the war in the South was the battered physical condition of the region. Many major cities had been reduced to rubble by fire and constant shelling from Union artillery.

Black men enlisted in the Union army during the Civil War.

Northern and Southern Resources, 1860[1,2]

Resources in 1860	North	South
Total population	22,300,000	9,100,000
Value of goods manufactured	$1.7 billion	$156 million
Railroad mileage	22,000 (35,400 km)	9,000 (14,500 km)
Coal production (tons)	13.6 million (12.3 metric tons)	650,000 (590,000 metric tons)
Corn and wheat production (bushels)	698 million	314 million
Cotton production (bales)	43,000	5.3 million
Men of military age (18-45)	3.5 million	1 million

At the start of the Civil War, Northern states were becoming increasingly industrialized while the South remained predominantly agricultural. Northern manufacturers produced more cotton and woolen textiles, leather goods, raw iron, and, importantly, more firearms than their Southern counterparts.

Richmond, Virginia, the capital of the Confederacy, lay in ruins. Bridges and roads had been destroyed, factories had been demolished, and hundreds of miles of railroad track had been torn apart by Union forces.

Agricultural production also fell victim to the ravages of war. Fields were torn up and plantations were overrun with weeds. In many places, land reduced in value. Many farmers could not afford to keep their property and were forced to sell their land at cheap prices. By the end of the war, Southern farmers were barely able to produce enough food to feed the inhabitants of the region.

Lawlessness and Disorder in the Postwar South

While federal officials debated how new state governments would be established in the South, law and order collapsed in many places throughout the region. Attacks by whites and former Confederate soldiers on freedmen were common. "In many instances negroes who walked away from the plantations, or were found upon the roads, were shot or otherwise severely punished," wrote journalist and later US senator Carl Schurz. "The impulse to whip a negro [is] almost irresistible," he continued. "It will continue to be so until the southern people will have learned, so as never to forget it, that a black man has rights which a white man is bound to respect."[3]

Hundreds of thousands of white refugees, displaced from their homes during the fighting, wandered over the land. Hundreds of thousands of newly freed black people were also on the move. Unemployment and crime were rampant. In most instances, federal troops occupying the conquered South were the only source of law and order.

Infrastructure and Economy

By 1870, much of the South's infrastructure was rebuilt and manufacturing output returned to prewar levels. However, some Southern states suffered lingering economic devastation. Mississippi went from being one of the nation's wealthiest states to one of the poorest, where it remains in the 2010s. In modern times, some of the poorest states in the United States, based on median household income, are those that seceded from the Union in 1861.

Into the 1900s, the Southern economy lagged far behind that of the booming North. By the mid-1900s, the South experienced improved economic fortunes. Low taxes, relaxed business regulations, and a large workforce lured many Northern companies to relocate southward. By the end of the century, job growth in the South's private sector outpaced that of every state that had fought for the Union.

In 2017, Mississippi had the highest poverty rate in the United States, followed closely by Louisiana.

Money and Labor Problems in the South

The South's problems were further worsened by money and labor woes. During the conflict, the Confederate states issued their own paper money to help pay for the war. With the collapse of the Confederacy, the notes became worthless. The lack of reliable cash fueled the South's already high prices for everyday goods and commodities, triggering an inflation that threatened to completely undermine the Southern recovery. The South desperately needed cash to get back on its feet and revive its shaken economy.

Where would the money come from? Some determined Northern entrepreneurs bought Southern land at devalued prices and began farming. Most of the farms failed, however, due to the same problems that plagued Southern farmers: bad weather, insect infestations, and high interest rates on borrowed money. Other Northern businessmen invested in Southern railroads, coalfields, and lumber companies.

Perhaps the South's most daunting challenge to resurrect its economy was solving its labor woes. With the emancipation of blacks, the South had lost the foundation of its economy: enslaved people. Abolition meant Southern farmers could no longer enslave human beings and force them to work, and these farmers now had to pay their workers. In addition, slaves had been property, and slaveholders could sell them to raise money. In the postwar South, slaveholders had lost a critical means of income. The loss of slave labor in the South soon led to conflict between farmers and former slaves. While former slaves were eager to establish their economic liberty, former slaveholders were equally motivated to keep them subservient.

In short, centuries of economic and social traditions, particularly the relationship between whites and enslaved blacks, had been upended. People wondered whether the federal government would seize property from white Southern landowners and redistribute it to freedmen.

The Southern economy had relied on slave labor for decades.

They also questioned whether freedmen would agree to work for former slaveholders.

The Victorious North

During the war, production increased in nearly every part of the Union economy. The development of mechanical reapers allowed Northern farmers to plant and harvest more crops faster and more efficiently than ever before. Thousands of manufacturers also thrived. Northern industries such as iron and steel production, petroleum, textiles, and leather goods expanded over the course of the war.

Railroad construction boomed. Developed in part to help transport Union troops and supplies, railroads also gave farmers and manufacturers a boost. The railroads allowed farmers to ship their goods to distant domestic markets in the east and west. The spread of the rail system spurred the growth of major cities such as Chicago, Illinois. By the end of the war, the US railroad system was the largest in the world.

Postwar Government

With their secession from the Union, Southern states had no representation in Congress. Powerless, their fate lay in the hands of the triumphant North.

Freedmen and the North

By 1804, all Northern states had passed laws to abolish slavery within their states. However, emancipation was gradual, and slavery still existed in some Northern states into the early 1860s. Racism was widespread in the North, as it was in the South. Free blacks faced discrimination in all parts of their lives, including employment, education, and the use of public facilities. Throughout the Union, blacks were denied the right to vote and were banned from testifying in court against whites.

A Union victory in the Civil War assured the emancipation of enslaved people. It also sparked optimism among free blacks with a sense of hope for better days ahead. During the early years of the war, a black freedman wrote:

Everything among us indicates a change in our condition. . . . Old things are passing away, and eventually old prejudices must follow. The revolution has begun, and time alone must decide where it is to end.[5]

The Republican Party, the political party of President Abraham Lincoln, controlled the federal government and most Northern state governments. Republicans favored abolition and opposed the spread of slavery to US territories in the west. Northern Republicans viewed the Union victory as an opportunity for the federal government to use its power to reshape and improve Southern society. Northern and Southern Democrats generally opposed federal intervention in state affairs and were less eager to embrace black emancipation and equality with whites. Despite opposition from Democrats, congressional Republicans, especially those in the North, would determine the nature of Reconstruction. The Republicans, however, were divided on a plan. This disagreement set in motion a tense battle between the executive branch and Congress—one that would permanently affect the course of US history.

DISCUSSION STARTERS

- The Civil War was mostly fought in the South and in western territories of the United States. Why do you think fewer battles were fought in the North?

- What do you think was the biggest factor in the Union winning the Civil War?

- Why do you think the majority of today's poorest US states are in the South?

CHAPTER THREE

PRESIDENTIAL RECONSTRUCTION

As early as the spring of 1861, President Lincoln began implementing plans to reunite the nation and establish governments in Southern areas that had been seized by Union armies. Lincoln claimed the Southern states did not have the right to secede, and therefore he did not recognize the Confederate government. Lincoln also maintained he was the sole authority to determine the course of resuming normal relations with the South.

THE PRESIDENT ACTS

Lincoln faced opposition from Radical Republicans in Congress. Radicals believed black people were entitled to the same freedoms, political rights, and opportunities as whites. Moderate and conservative

Republicans encouraged President Lincoln to free enslaved people.

Republicans opposed slavery but did not support equal rights for blacks. When Congress met in the winter of 1861–1862, Radical Republicans, including Senator Charles Sumner of Massachusetts, introduced bills that declared Congress, not Lincoln, the sole authority to set the terms of Reconstruction of the South. Radicals also insisted that the terms included seizing the Confederates' lands and temporarily limiting their legal rights. The bills passed but were not strictly enforced.

In 1863, Lincoln issued the Emancipation Proclamation, which freed all enslaved people living in the Confederacy. In addition, on December 8, 1863, Lincoln issued the Proclamation of Amnesty and Reconstruction, also known as the Ten Percent Plan. The president's plan addressed three issues. First, it granted full amnesty and restored

the property to those
involved in the rebellion,
with the exception of
some high-ranking civilian
and military Confederate
officers. Second, it
allowed for a new state
government to be formed
when 10 percent of all
eligible voters in the state's
1860 census had taken
an oath of allegiance to
the United States. Third,
readmitted states had to
adopt a state constitution
abolishing slavery.

Congressional
Republicans approved
Lincoln's requirement of abolition for readmission, but
they were not satisfied with the plan's other terms, which
they viewed as lenient and charitable. Radicals objected
to the restoration of political rights and Confederate
lands. In addition, the proclamation allowed for state
governments to be formed before voters approved new
state constitutions.

Once in operation, "Nowhere in the Confederacy did Lincoln's new program produce the results he sought," wrote historian David Herbert Donald.[2] Not a single state was readmitted to the Union during the war. New loyal state governments established in occupied territories in Louisiana, Arkansas, and Tennessee won Lincoln's approval, but each failed to produce a state government that satisfied the Republican members of Congress. Many Radical Republicans believed the governments held antiblack views and that Lincoln's lenient oath of allegiance was an insufficient test of loyalty to the Union.

THE WADE-DAVIS BILL

In the spring of 1864, Congress conceived its first detailed plan of Reconstruction. In July, a bill written by Senator Benjamin Wade of Ohio and Representative Henry Winter Davis of Maryland passed in Congress. The Wade-Davis Bill set forth stricter terms of Reconstruction than Lincoln's.

The bill had several main goals. First, it called for temporary military governors who were loyal to the Union to be appointed in the states that had seceded. These governors were to oversee restoration. Second, a majority of a state's white citizens had to swear an oath of loyalty to the United States before a constitutional convention could be called. A constitutional convention is a gathering of political representatives for the purpose of writing a

Benjamin Wade was a strong opponent of slavery.

new constitution or amending an existing one. In addition, each person would be required to take an oath that he had never voluntarily given aid to the Confederacy. Each state constitution was to disqualify ex-Confederate officials from voting or holding office. New state constitutions would also need to abolish slavery and renounce secession.

Lincoln refused to sign the bill. He worried it would undo whatever progress was being made in the test states working under his Ten Percent Plan. He also believed slavery should be abolished not by a federal law but rather by an amendment to the Constitution. Despite their differences, by January 31, 1865, Lincoln and the

Radical Republicans obtained congressional approval for the Thirteenth Amendment, which abolished slavery throughout the Union.

On the evening of April 14, 1865, Lincoln was assassinated at Ford's Theatre in Washington, DC. His killer was John Wilkes Booth, a Confederate sympathizer living in the North during the Civil War. At the time of Lincoln's death, neither he nor Congress had a fixed plan for the South. Lincoln's successor, Andrew Johnson, would take the reins of Reconstruction.

JOHNSON'S RECONSTRUCTION

Johnson was a Southerner and a Democrat. Born in North Carolina, Johnson favored states' rights, and although he opposed secession, he did not oppose slavery. In fact, Johnson owned slaves, but not while he was president.

Like Lincoln, Johnson believed Southerners should choose their own state governments without federal government intervention. He, too, believed that Reconstruction was the president's responsibility.

Days after taking office, Johnson spoke harshly against the defeated Confederates. "They must not only be punished, but their social power must be destroyed," he told an audience in Indiana.[3] To a group of congressmen that included Pennsylvania Radical Republican Thaddeus Stevens, the president exclaimed, "To those . . . who

President Johnson was a supporter of states' rights.

attempted to destroy the life of the nation—I would say, on you be inflicted the severest penalties of your crime."[4] Johnson's tough words appealed to the Radical Republicans, who preferred the new president's firm stance toward the South over Lincoln's perceived generous attitude.

However, Johnson's statements were never put into action. In May 1865, Johnson issued his policy for Amnesty and Reconstruction. By taking an oath of loyalty to the Union, all males in the Confederacy—excluding military officers and political leaders—would be pardoned and be able to vote and hold office. The plan also called for appointed provisional governors to reorganize each state's political affairs. Once the newly elected state government officials and congressmen ratified the Thirteenth Amendment, banning slavery, the state would be ready for readmission to the Union. Johnson hoped to work with Southern leaders who were loyal to the Union. He opposed the idea of giving control of Southern governments to either blacks or staunch anti-Confederates.

UNEXPECTED CONSEQUENCES

When Southern white voters went to the polls in the summer and fall of 1865, they failed to live up to Johnson's expectations. Voters elected dozens of high-ranking Confederate military officers and public officials as governors, state legislators, and US congressmen. Confederate states held conventions and wrote new constitutions, but some refused to ratify the Thirteenth Amendment.

Eager to complete Reconstruction as hastily as possible, Johnson backed down. He ordered all land seized by the Union army to be returned to its Confederate owners. He also began withdrawing Union forces from the South and granted thousands of pardons to men who were originally excluded from his Amnesty and Reconstruction proclamation.

Why did Johnson abandon his plan? One reason was his prejudice toward blacks. To a White House visitor, the president remarked, "White men alone must manage the South."[5] Another reason Johnson yielded to the unexpected consequences of his Reconstruction plan was to keep the support of Southern voters so he could win reelection in 1868.

Most congressional Republicans were outraged at what was happening in the South. Ex-Confederates were again running state governments and making no attempt to protect the rights of African Americans, despite Johnson's order to the contrary. By the end of 1865, deadly attacks on black people by whites had, according to Donald, "reached epidemic proportions."[6]

BLACK CODES

Starting in November 1865, Southern governments began enacting a series of discriminatory laws known as Black Codes. Blacks were prohibited from renting farmland. African Americans had to sign yearly work contracts, and unemployed blacks could be fined, imprisoned, or forced to work without pay. The codes barred black people from any occupation other than farmer. And in some states, black people were prohibited from hunting, fishing, and owning guns.

Many black people protested this type of reenslavement. In one instance, on November 24, 1865, a group of black delegates met in Charleston, South Carolina, to demand full rights as US citizens and to strike down the oppressive Black Codes. In a written statement directed at white South Carolinians, the delegation declared:

> You have by your Legislative actions placed barriers in the way of our educational and mechanical improvement. . . . We simply desire that we shall be recognized as men; that we have no obstructions placed in our way; that the same laws which govern white men shall direct colored men.[7]

Like the appeals of other African Americans who demanded the repeal of Black Codes, the delegation's request fell on deaf ears. White Southern police forces and court systems oversaw the application of the Black Codes. It was a racist and discriminatory system "in which blacks enjoyed virtually no voice whatever," according to historian Eric Foner.[8] In short, the state governments established under Johnson's policies were doing all in their power to ensure white dominance in the South during the postwar era.

The racist style of Confederate Reconstruction convinced Republicans and Northerners that Johnson's plan had failed. They argued that changes in Reconstruction policy were desperately needed. When Congress met in 1865, the Radical Republicans decided to challenge Johnson and take matters into their own hands.

DISCUSSION STARTERS

- Imagine you lived in the North after the Civil War. How would you feel about Southerners and the treatment the South should receive during Reconstruction?

- If Lincoln had not been killed, do you think he would have been able to work with Radical Republicans and compromise on a plan for Reconstruction? Explain your answer.

- What discriminatory policies exist throughout the United States today? How are they similar to the Black Codes?

CHAPTER FOUR

CONGRESS PUSHES BACK

The Southern black community did not sit idly as the Black Codes and antiblack Southern governments continued to restrict their freedoms. Blacks wrote to their state legislatures, expressing their desire for equal treatment with whites. They established Equal Rights Leagues to protest oppression by local officials and businesses. Blacks also broke away from racially mixed churches and established their own houses of worship, places that would become social and cultural centers for African Americans.

As blacks remained vigilant in their fight for civil rights, events were heating up in Congress. By late 1865, Radical Republicans, led by Stevens and Sumner, demanded that Johnson's Southern

African Americans participated in conventions to fight for equal rights.

governments be dissolved and replaced with new ones selected by white and black voters. Johnson strongly opposed the Radicals' position. When Congress assembled in December, the general body of Republicans refused to recognize and seat the representatives from Johnson's Southern governments. The Republicans had directly challenged Johnson's presidential authority and left no doubt that they rejected his program of Reconstruction.

An Investigation Begins

Prompted by Radicals, Congress established the Joint Committee on Reconstruction to investigate the new Southern governments and report whether any of them should be represented in Congress. Until a report was made, no member of the investigated governments was to be seated. The committee was largely interested in gathering information about the treatment of black people and Northerners by white Southerners.

Only three of the 15 members on the committee were Democrats.[1] The committee heard testimony from 144 witnesses, including Northerners living in the South, former slaves, and white Southerners, both Unionist and pro-Confederate.[2] Among the Northerners were agents of the Freedmen's Bureau, which aimed to help former slaves and poor whites in the South after the Civil War, and US army officers.

Thaddeus Stevens proposed to Congress that the Joint Committee on Reconstruction be created.

The testimonies revealed widespread hostility and mistreatment of black people in the South. Reports of freedmen being shot and black women and workers being tortured filled the pages of the 1866 report. One black witness from Virginia stated, "In Surrey County, they are taking the colored people and tying them up by the thumbs if they do not agree to work for six dollars a month."[3]

The committee's findings blasted Johnson's governments, proclaiming, "The question before Congress is, then, whether conquered enemies have the right, and shall be permitted at their own pleasure and on their own terms, to participate in making laws for their conquerors."[4]

In light of the testimonies, Congress generated two bills in 1866. The first was a bill to extend the life and increase the functions of the Freedmen's Bureau, which was scheduled to expire shortly. The second was a Civil Rights Bill, which declared all persons born in the United States national citizens.

Johnson vetoed both bills. He claimed the Freedmen's Bureau infringed on states' rights, illegally gave aid to a particular group of people at the exclusion of others, and was too expensive. Democrats and moderate Republicans praised the president's veto. But in July, Congress passed a revised Freedmen's Bureau bill over another Johnson veto, extending the life of the agency for two more years.

Johnson vetoed the Civil Rights Bill, claiming it created "safeguards" for people of color "which go indefinitely beyond any that the General Government has ever provided for the white race . . . the distinction of race and color is by the bill made to operate in favor of the colored against the white race."[5] Johnson's veto of the Civil Rights Bill indicated he had no intention of authorizing the federal government to protect blacks' civil rights.

With near unanimous Republican support, in April Congress overrode Johnson's veto, and the Civil Rights Bill of 1866 became law. Johnson's uncompromising attitude on his Reconstruction policies damaged his relationship with Republicans, including moderates.

In 1866, a white supremacist government candidate used a political cartoon to attack the idea of black suffrage.

THE FOURTEENTH AMENDMENT

Radicals and moderates agreed to formulate a constitutional amendment that satisfied each of their main goals. The Radicals wanted to grant black men the right to vote, while the moderates wanted an amendment that seceded states had to ratify before readmission to the Union.

The Fourteenth Amendment stated that anyone born in the United States was a citizen and had the rights of a citizen. This clause ensured that the freedmen were officially US citizens and had the same constitutional rights as any US citizen. The amendment did not specifically give black men the right to vote. Instead, it left that decision to the states. However, if a state denied any group of men the right to vote, it would lose some of its representatives in Congress. Radicals were displeased because they felt the amendment did not provide sufficient guarantees of voting rights for blacks.

Johnson opposed the amendment on the grounds that the Constitution should not be changed without representation from the Southern states. He also believed ratification should not be a condition of readmission to the Union. Nevertheless, Congress approved the Fourteenth Amendment in June 1866, sending it to the states for approval. Most Southern states refused to ratify it. The federal government held firm and denied the Southern states representation in Congress until they voted for ratification. The Fourteenth Amendment was eventually added to the Constitution in 1868.

RACE RIOTS

Incidents of racial violence during the spring and summer of 1866 fueled increasing public doubt over Johnson's Reconstruction policies. From May 1 to May 3, white mobs, assisted by local police officers and firemen, assaulted black people on the streets of Memphis, Tennessee. The attacks ended only when General George Stoneman, commander of white and black federal troops in the area, established order. Nearly 50 people, mostly black, were killed, and about 285 were wounded.[6] Hundreds of black schools, churches, and homes were burned or looted.

Two months later, on July 30, violence erupted in New Orleans, Louisiana. At the city's constitutional convention, where Unionists hoped to gain black suffrage and launch a new state government, white people fired on unarmed black and white delegates and their supporters. Many victims who surrendered were killed on the spot. Aided by local police, the attackers killed dozens of black people and wounded even more. The two violent episodes energized national opposition to Johnson's policies.

US general Philip Sheridan was a Civil War hero and an outspoken critic of Johnson's Reconstruction policies. Sheridan went to New Orleans after the July 1866 riot. He wrote to Johnson and General Ulysses S. Grant to inform the two men about conditions in the city. Sheridan said that the city's police force had attacked members of the constitutional convention and black supporters, "in a manner so unnecessary and atrocious as to compel me to say that it was murder."[7] In a reply to Sheridan, Johnson called the convention "illegal and unauthorized proceedings, intended and calculated to upturn the existing State Government of Louisiana."[8]

Women's Rights and the Fourteenth Amendment

During the Civil War, the movement for women's suffrage was largely interrupted, with most women's rights advocates supporting the Union cause and equal rights for black people. When the Fourteenth Amendment was proposed, many women's rights activists were outraged. For the first time, the word *male* was used in the Constitution. A section of the amendment declared that all male citizens over the age of 21 were eligible to vote, asserting that only men had that right.

Black women found themselves oppressed for both their status as women and their race. By the late 1800s, black women suffragists organized to gain the right to vote. In 1869, Charlotte Forten Grimké founded the National Association of Colored Women. In 1913, Ida B. Wells founded the Alpha Suffrage Club of Chicago.

The Fifteenth Amendment, adopted in 1870, guaranteed protection against racial discrimination in voting. The new law applied only to men, meaning women—both colored and white—still did not have the right to vote. The Nineteenth Amendment, adopted in 1920, stated that US citizens could not be denied the right to vote on the basis of sex. Yet many black people, particularly in the South, were discouraged from voting by being made to pay new taxes or take comprehension tests regarding the US Constitution. The Voting Rights Act of 1965 finally outlawed all discriminatory voting practices, clearing the way for universal black suffrage.

Ida B. Wells helped organize black women in their fight for suffrage.

JOHNSON RALLIES SUPPORT

In response to growing opposition, Johnson's supporters convened the National Union Convention, which met in Philadelphia on August 14, 1866. The goal of the convention was to rally support for Johnson's lenient Reconstruction policies and create a new political party that was amenable to his strategy. In the end, the convention failed to establish a new national party. Johnson decided to take his case directly to the American people.

On August 28, Johnson embarked on a speaking tour in hopes of regaining public support. Another aim of the tour was to encourage voters to elect congressmen in the upcoming 1866 elections who would support his policies. Johnson traveled throughout the North. He visited New York City and Baltimore, Maryland, and then went through upstate New York and west to Cleveland, Ohio; Detroit, Michigan; Chicago; and other cities.

The tour was a dismal failure. During his speeches, the president used foul and abusive language to attack his Republican opponents. Johnson accused Radical Republicans of intentionally starting the riot in New Orleans. In many cities, Johnson responded to hecklers, who turned out in the hundreds to challenge him. In Cleveland, one person yelled "Hang Jeff Davis [president of the Confederacy]!" Johnson angrily said, "Why not hang Thad Stevens and Wendell Phillips [an abolitionist]?"[9]

Johnson's confrontational style alienated Northern audiences and newspapers. Republicans were particularly angered by Johnson's claim that they encouraged black violence in the South. In the end, Johnson lost most of the support he had in the North. In the 1866 congressional elections, the Republicans maintained two-thirds majorities in both the Senate and the House of Representatives and were in complete control of the governments of every Northern state and three of the border states. The president had all but handed the reins of Reconstruction to his Republican opponents. From this point forward, Congress, not Johnson, would drive Reconstruction policy.

CONGRESSIONAL RECONSTRUCTION

Fresh off their victories in the 1866 congressional elections, Republicans immediately introduced new legislation to change the course of Johnson's policies. The primary goals of the legislation were to ensure black rights in the South and replace the president's Southern governments. In January 1867, Congress overrode a veto by Johnson, granting voting rights to all adult male citizens of the District of Columbia, including black men.

MILITARY RECONSTRUCTION ACTS

Riding a crest of self-confidence, Radical Republicans pressed their agenda to reshape Reconstruction. On March 2, 1867, Radical and moderate Republicans passed the first of four

Many African American men sought out their right to vote.

VOTERS

Military Reconstruction Acts, each over Johnson's veto. The stricter terms of the Reconstruction Acts attempted to force black suffrage on the South, thereby eroding white Southerners' political grip on the region.

The first act divided the South into five military districts to be overseen by military governors until new state constitutions were created and approved by Congress. Johnson's state governments were now accountable to US military authority. All males, including blacks but not leading Confederate officials, were to participate in the constitutional conventions. Southern states had to ratify the Fourteenth Amendment in order to be readmitted to the Union.

The period of so-called Radical Reconstruction had begun and would last until 1877. Congress passed three additional Military Reconstruction Acts (two in 1867 and one in 1868), which outlined how state constitutions were to be created and approved.

Congress needed the military to carry out its plan, and therefore it decided to end Johnson's control of the US army as commander in chief. Republicans included a clause in the third act that gave ultimate power to the army generals supervising each of the five districts in the South. The generals were granted the authority to remove any official from office in their districts if they believed he

Radical Republicans were largely in charge of writing the
Reconstruction Acts.

was hindering the process of Reconstruction. The generals
were also forbidden to take orders from any civilian
official in the federal government.

THE STRUGGLE FOR CONTROL

On the same day they passed the first Military
Reconstruction Act, congressional Republicans passed two
additional laws to pull control of the army from Johnson.
The Tenure of Office Act was passed to prevent the
president from removing appointed federal officials, such

as cabinet members, without the approval of the Senate. The Republicans made the move to prevent Johnson from removing major officials who supported the Radicals.

Congress also passed the Army Appropriations Act, which stated that the nation's general-in-chief—the military officer in charge of the armed forces—could not be removed or relocated from his headquarters in Washington, DC, without the approval of the Senate. At the time, General Ulysses S. Grant, a Republican, held the position. Significantly, the act also required that any order issued to the US army be done only through the general-in-chief. Orders not sent through him were invalid. In short, Congress prohibited the president from issuing orders directly to the army.

To combat bold moves made by Congress, Johnson decided to strike back by using his power of removal. Federal law allowed a president to remove an appointed official when the Senate was not in session. On August 5, 1867, while Congress was in recess, Johnson demanded Secretary of War Edwin Stanton's resignation. Stanton was a critic of the president's Reconstruction policies and a strong advocate for black civil rights. When Stanton refused, Johnson suspended him and appointed General Grant as temporary secretary of war.

Some people believed the Tenure of Office Act was created in part to protect Edwin Stanton's position.

IMPEACHMENT PROCEEDINGS

Republicans were outraged, arguing that Johnson had violated the Tenure of Office Act. In January 1868, the Senate reinstated Stanton, but Johnson was determined to win this battle. In February, the president fired Stanton and notified Congress that he was appointing General Lorenzo Thomas as temporary secretary of war. Senate Republicans immediately charged Johnson with direct violation of the Tenure of Office Act. On February 24, 1868, the House of Representatives voted to impeach the president by a count of 126 to 47.[1] Every Republican voted in favor of impeachment; every Democrat voted against it.

One week later, the House adopted articles of impeachment. Most of the charges related to Johnson's violation of removing Stanton and appointing Thomas without the approval of Congress. The impeachment trial formally began in the Senate on March 11. On May 16 and again on May 26, the Senate voted on the charges. Both times the vote was 35 for guilty and 19 for not guilty— one vote short of the two-thirds majority necessary for removal from office.[2] Johnson promised he would no longer oppose congressional Reconstruction and served out the balance of his term in office, nine months, keeping his word.

THE NEW SOUTH?

By the fall of 1867, the ex-Confederate states were working to meet the demands imposed on them by Congress in order to be readmitted to the Union. However, many Southerners resented Northern intervention in their affairs. Ex-Confederate Democrats actively opposed the new constitutional conventions and ratification of the Fourteenth Amendment, sometimes with violence and intimidation.

But with newfound hope, black men came to the polls in 1867 to exercise their first taste of political power. Black men made up the majority of all Southern Republican voters, but only Louisiana, Mississippi, and South Carolina had a majority of black voters. During Reconstruction, an estimated 2,000 African Americans were voted into public office, from local officials to governor to US senator.[3]

Despite the remarkable burst of African American political involvement, black people never dominated Southern Republican governments, and in some states they were vastly underrepresented. In Texas, North Carolina, and Georgia, whites held overwhelmingly large majorities of the legislative seats. African Americans' greatest success was on the local level as commissioners, counselors, and sheriffs. Southern whites were angered and unnerved by armed black law enforcement officers.

Black political leaders came from all walks of life. Many were former slaves who rose to become teachers, artisans, ministers, and abolitionists. Others were born into freedom and were educated at the new black colleges established during Reconstruction.

Hundreds of black people headed Union Leagues. By 1867, leagues had formed in some parts of the South. Boasting interracial membership, the leagues raised money for black schools and churches, gave aid to the sick and needy, and fought for desegregated public facilities. League members also organized strikes against unfair white employers and demanded the right to sit on local juries. The leagues' primary function, according to historian Eric Foner, was political education. Union Leagues urged black people to vote, sponsored candidates for office, and educated African Americans on the political issues of the day.

African Americans' improved position in Southern society came at a steep price. Black officeholders faced the threat of violence daily. Roughly one-tenth of all black members of the 1867 and 1868 state constitutional conventions were victims of white violence. Seven black delegates were murdered.[5] Other local leaders were savagely whipped, while ordinary black citizens were threatened with violence if

On October 29, 1869, members of the Ku Klux Klan (KKK) burst into the home of Abram Colby of Greene County, Georgia, dragged him out, and severely beat him. Colby, a former slave who was elected to the Georgia House of Representatives, was nearly killed in the savage attack. In testimony to a senate committee, Colby said, "[The Klansmen] took me to the woods and whipped me three hours or more and left me for dead." Colby's daughter was in the room when the intruders came. "My little daughter begged them not to carry me away," he said.[6] Colby added that the KKK pulled a gun on his daughter, terrifying her.

they tried to vote at local polls. White Republicans were also the victims of violence and murder.

CARPETBAGGERS AND SCALAWAGS

In most Southern states, the Republican Party required the votes of both black and white people to gain political power. Republican governance required a coalition of African Americans and two newly formed groups of whites: carpetbaggers and scalawags.

Carpetbagger was a scornful term used by Southerners to describe white Northerners who moved to the South to purchase land or go into business with Southern planters. White Republicans born in the South were known to their foes as scalawags. Most scalawags were nonslaveholding small farmers who generally did not support secession. Some joined the Union army. Many were harassed and intimidated for their Union sympathies by other Southerners and Confederate officials. Scalawags hoped to prevent former Confederate leadership from regaining power in the South.

THE CONSTITUTIONAL CONVENTIONS

Republican majorities at the 1867–1869 constitutional conventions drafted new state constitutions. Southern blacks and so-called carpetbaggers and scalawags formed the majority of delegates. African Americans made up the

majority of delegates in South Carolina and Louisiana, but whites accounted for 55 percent of the total number of delegates. Of the 265 black men in ten state constitutional conventions, roughly 107 had been born slaves.[7]

In general, the new state constitutions reflected the overall Republican agenda. The constitutions guaranteed African Americans civil and political rights, established systems of public education, and called for the creation of hospitals and institutions to care for orphans and the mentally ill. Black delegates and carpetbaggers voted down segregation in schools and other public facilities, but no constitution required integration.

Southern Democrats, frustrated and angered by the Republicans' dominance at the conventions, lashed out at their enemies. Alabama newspaper editors warned that black delegates would "Africanize" the state, while a South Carolina paper claimed, "Southern [whites] do not intend to be mongrelized."[8]

THE ACHIEVEMENTS OF RECONSTRUCTION

The early years of Reconstruction brought much change to the South. One of the most notable reforms was the establishment of the first state-funded public education systems in the region. Blacks in particular benefited from this. By 1900, the African American literacy rate was 55 percent, compared with 21 percent in 1870.[9] Black schools and universities produced teachers, doctors, skilled workers, and other professionals.

Civil rights protection improved. New state constitutions outlawed the Black Codes, and laws were passed to ensure black farmworkers were paid for their work. Discrimination was never entirely erased, but black people gained greater employment opportunities during

Reconstruction. Once banned from public service jobs, African Americans served in police and fire departments, worked as justices of the peace, and held public office.

As a means to reenergize the Southern economy, Republican governments promoted railroad construction. At first it was a promising undertaking. But financially struggling railroads demanded aid, which took state funds from projects such as schools and hospitals. When the railroads were unable to pay back the debts, state governments were forced to raise taxes to make good on the borrowed money. In the end, the problems caused by railroad difficulties and other factors would contribute to the collapse of Radical Reconstruction and the Republican Party's loss of congressional power.

DISCUSSION STARTERS

- Do you think Congress was right in taking power away from President Johnson? Explain your reasoning.

- Johnson escaped removal by one vote. Describe what might have happened if Johnson had been forced to leave office.

- Why do you think some white people were violent toward black people during Reconstruction?

CHAPTER SIX

THE TIDE TURNS

By May 1868, no Southern state, with the exception of Tennessee, had ratified the Fourteenth Amendment—a critical condition of the seceded states' readmission to the Union. Violence toward freedmen, carpetbaggers, and scalawags threatened the terms of the Reconstruction Acts. Resentment among white Southerners over black rights and Northern interference in the affairs of the South were reaching a boiling point.

THE RISE OF THE KU KLUX KLAN

In 1868, the secretly organized group known as the Ku Klux Klan (KKK) launched a campaign of violence and intimidation aimed mainly against freedmen. The KKK had three goals: to crush

During Reconstruction, Union soldiers stayed in cities such as Atlanta to maintain peace.

the black vote by preventing African Americans from registering to vote and going to the polls, destroy the Republican governments in the South, and restore white supremacy.

The growth of the KKK in Tennessee, North Carolina, and Alabama spurred the formation of other antiblack groups. Louisiana had the Knights of the White Camellia, Texas had the Knights of the Rising, and Mississippi had the White Line. Dozens of similar groups sprang up throughout the South. Their common goal was to undo the changes of Reconstruction. Their common means to accomplish this were violence and terror against black people and their white supporters.

Many African Americans fled their hometowns to escape the KKK. William Coleman, living in Macon, Mississippi, was one of many who experienced Klan violence. Eight Klansmen, all wearing disguises, broke into Coleman's house and beat him mercilessly. Coleman said his attackers "whipped me until I couldn't move or holler or nothing, but just lay there like a log. . . . They left me there for dead."[1]

Few individuals who supported Reconstruction were safe from Klan harassment. Klansmen attacked black and white members and officials of the Union Leagues and the Freedmen's Bureau. Much of the group's violence in 1868

The KKK targeted many people who were not white Protestants.

was intended to assist the Democratic Party and prevent Republican Ulysses S. Grant from winning the presidential election in November. By the time the election rolled around, all but four of the seceded states had been restored to the Union and could vote. Texas, Virginia, Mississippi, and Georgia had not met the conditions of readmission to the Union and therefore could not vote in the election. It wasn't until July 1870 that all of the former Confederate states were readmitted to the Union.

Grant won the election, but the KKK's terrorism prevented many black people from voting or frightened them into voting for the Democratic candidate, Horatio Seymour. Grant's opponent won in Louisiana and Georgia. Historian Allen W. Trelease concluded that through intimidation and the resultant suppression of black

African American Politician Tunis Campbell

Tunis Campbell was one of the most successful and high-ranking black politicians during Reconstruction. Born in New Jersey in 1812 to free parents, Campbell attended an otherwise all-white religious school in Long Island, New York. Campbell became an outspoken abolitionist lecturer. After working as a missionary in the New York–New Jersey area, he moved to Boston to manage a hotel. In 1863, Secretary of War Edwin Stanton commissioned Campbell to work on South Carolina's Sea Islands to help black people who were settling in the region.

Two years later, Campbell worked for the Freedmen's Bureau, where he organized black settlements on several islands off the coast of Georgia. Campbell then purchased acreage on Georgia's mainland in McIntosh County and leased land to black farmers. Black voters helped elect Campbell to the Georgia State Constitutional Convention, where he and fellow black delegates called for constitutional changes to benefit African Americans. In 1868, Campbell was elected to the Georgia Senate, working for equal education for blacks and fair voting regulations.

By that time, Campbell and hundreds of formerly enslaved people had established a thriving community on Georgia's Saint Catherine's Island. There, he served as justice of the peace and led a black militia to protect the area from KKK attacks. Campbell died in Boston, Massachusetts, in 1891 at age 79.

participation at the polls, the Klan served as "a terrorist arm of the Democratic Party, whether the party leaders as a whole like it or not."[2]

The Weakening Begins

By the early 1870s, political and social changes in the South began to endanger the Republican Party and congressional Reconstruction. Many of the Southern whites who held office opposed Radical initiatives such as full equality for blacks, establishing orphanages, and providing aid to railroads.

In addition, several of the leading Northern politicians who led Radical Reconstruction had died, leaving few powerful voices to press their agenda. Thaddeus Stevens died in 1868 and Charles Sumner in 1874. Senator Benjamin Wade of Ohio and Representative George Julian of Indiana failed to win reelection. Other Radical leaders began to

Struggling to Move Forward

In Georgia, during the spring elections of 1868, Democrats united with moderate Republicans to prevent the election of Radical candidates to the US Senate. A coalition of Democrats and moderates in the Georgia legislature also managed to expel all black legislators on the grounds that the new state constitution did not specifically give African Americans the right to hold office. Throughout the South, whites established black Democratic clubs to help split the black vote and weaken the Republican Party. To encourage participation in the clubs, whites often resorted to threats.

shift their efforts away from reshaping the South to overall national political reform and reconciliation with the ex-Confederates.

The Democrats worked hard to convince white voters throughout the country that Republicans were corrupt and incapable of governing effectively. One of the Democrats' favorite targets was the Radicals' railroad program. When the system became too expensive to run, Republicans were forced to raise taxes, placing a sizable burden on Southern taxpayers. In addition, several Republican legislators were found to be taking bribes from railroad companies.

The Democrats also attacked Republicans for the widespread corruption and scandal that rocked the Grant administration. During his first term as president, Grant's brother-in-law conspired with business tycoons James Fisk and Jay Gould to attempt to influence the government, corner the gold market, and drive up the price of that metal. The scheme failed and resulted in a financial panic on September 24, 1869, known as Black Friday. In another instance, Grant's private secretary, Orville Babcock, was accused of taking bribes to cheat the federal government out of millions of dollars in liquor taxes.

Democrats further appealed to dissatisfied Southern whites by exploiting antiblack attitudes. Democrats

Grant was not involved in any of the scandals during his presidency, but they tarnished his administration.

denounced blacks' political gains, declaring that African Americans should not have the right to vote or hold public office.

By the mid-1870s, the Democrats were on their way to toppling the Republicans and restoring white supremacy in the South. By 1877, the Democrats controlled all but three of the 11 formerly seceded states. Only South Carolina, Florida, and Louisiana remained in Republican hands. To protect their white power, many whites continued to discriminate and intimidate blacks. Tensions between the races mounted. Antiblack violence, segregation, and legal racial discrimination increased.

LOSING GROUND

Republicans' woes were compounded by a series of Supreme Court decisions that rolled back gains made during congressional Reconstruction. In 1873, in the Slaughterhouse Cases, the court ruled that the Fourteenth Amendment applied only to those rights spelled out in the Constitution. It applied only to the rights of national citizenship, not state citizenship, said the court. The rights of state citizenship were beyond federal protection. In effect, the ruling limited the Fourteenth Amendment's protection of privileges and supported the Jim Crow laws—a blow to freedmen and Republicans alike.

Two other cases affected how the federal government could enforce constitutional amendments. In *United States v. Cruikshank* in 1876, the court ruled that the Fourteenth Amendment empowered the federal government to act only against states when they violated a person's civil rights, not against individuals. The narrowing interpretation of the Fourteenth Amendment "made national prosecution of crimes committed against blacks almost impossible," according to Eric Foner.[3] Over time, the decision led to further violence against African Americans and the denial of their civil rights.

The case of *United States v. Reese* in 1876 was a test of the Fifteenth Amendment, which granted voting rights to black men. In this case, an African American man in Kentucky had been denied voting rights, and a voting official was charged with a crime under the Enforcement Act of 1870. The court ruled that the Enforcement Act of 1870, which forbade people from gathering together to violate others' rights, was unconstitutional. Under this ruling, Southern states began to legally impose literacy tests, poll taxes, and other restrictions to deny black people their right to vote.

The nation's economic conditions further weakened congressional Reconstruction. In 1873, the banking firm Jay Cooke and Company closed down.

The firm had helped finance the Union army during the Civil War and was heavily invested in railroads. The firm's collapse set off a chain reaction of other bank and industry closings. Unemployment skyrocketed, and the nation plunged into a long economic depression. Many people blamed President Grant and the Radical Republicans for the disaster.

RESISTANCE CONTINUES

As the nation's economic troubles deepened, many people in the North and South began to blame the failure of Reconstruction on emancipation and black rights. Southerners continued to turn to violence to topple Republican Reconstruction governments and intimidate blacks. In July 1876, mayhem erupted in the small town of Hamburg, South Carolina. Hamburg was an all-black community and predominantly Republican. As in many places throughout the postwar South, African Americans formed legal militias to keep the peace and maintain law and order in their areas. On July 4, two white farmers tried to travel on a main road in the town that was being used by the all-black militia during a training exercise. After a heated argument, the farmers managed to get through the militia's formation, but tension ran high: the fuse for racial violence had been lit.

Two days later, hundreds of armed whites stormed into Hamburg and chased the militiamen into a warehouse. After exchanges of gunfire, the vastly outnumbered militia members surrendered. Four of them were immediately murdered by the white mob. As others attempted to flee, the whites fired upon them. In all, six black people were murdered.[5] The governor of South Carolina asked for assistance from the federal government to arrest the whites who had attacked the militiamen. Federal government officials failed to respond, which undermined the authority of the state's Republican Party. Worse, it spurred more violence between blacks and whites in the South.

On December 24, 1865, a handful of ex-Confederate soldiers formed a social club. The group selected the name Ku Klux Klan (KKK), after the Greek word *kyklos*, meaning "circle." Within months, the group, disguised in white sheets and robes, began making nighttime rides through Southern black communities, intimidating and threatening local freedmen. Whippings and hangings of blacks became commonplace throughout the South. Klansmen drove thousands of black people from their homes and confiscated their land, livestock, and crops.

By 1920, the group's membership numbered 100,000. Within five years, as many as five million people belonged to the KKK, with millions of nonmember supporters.[6] The widespread popularity of the Klan may have been inspired in part by the 1915 silent film *The Birth of a Nation*, directed by D. W. Griffith. Hugely popular among white audiences, the film portrayed the KKK as a heroic group saving the South from Reconstruction-era freedmen. Blacks were defamed as ignorant, lazy, dangerous, and unruly. The three-hour movie sparked numerous protests in African American communities throughout the North, while the newly formed National Association for the Advancement of Colored People (NAACP) unsuccessfully tried to have the film banned.

Over time, the KKK's influence and political power in local and national affairs has ebbed and flowed. The civil rights movement ignited the fires of hate once again. Throughout the 1950s and 1960s, the KKK waged war on Southern blacks and white supporters

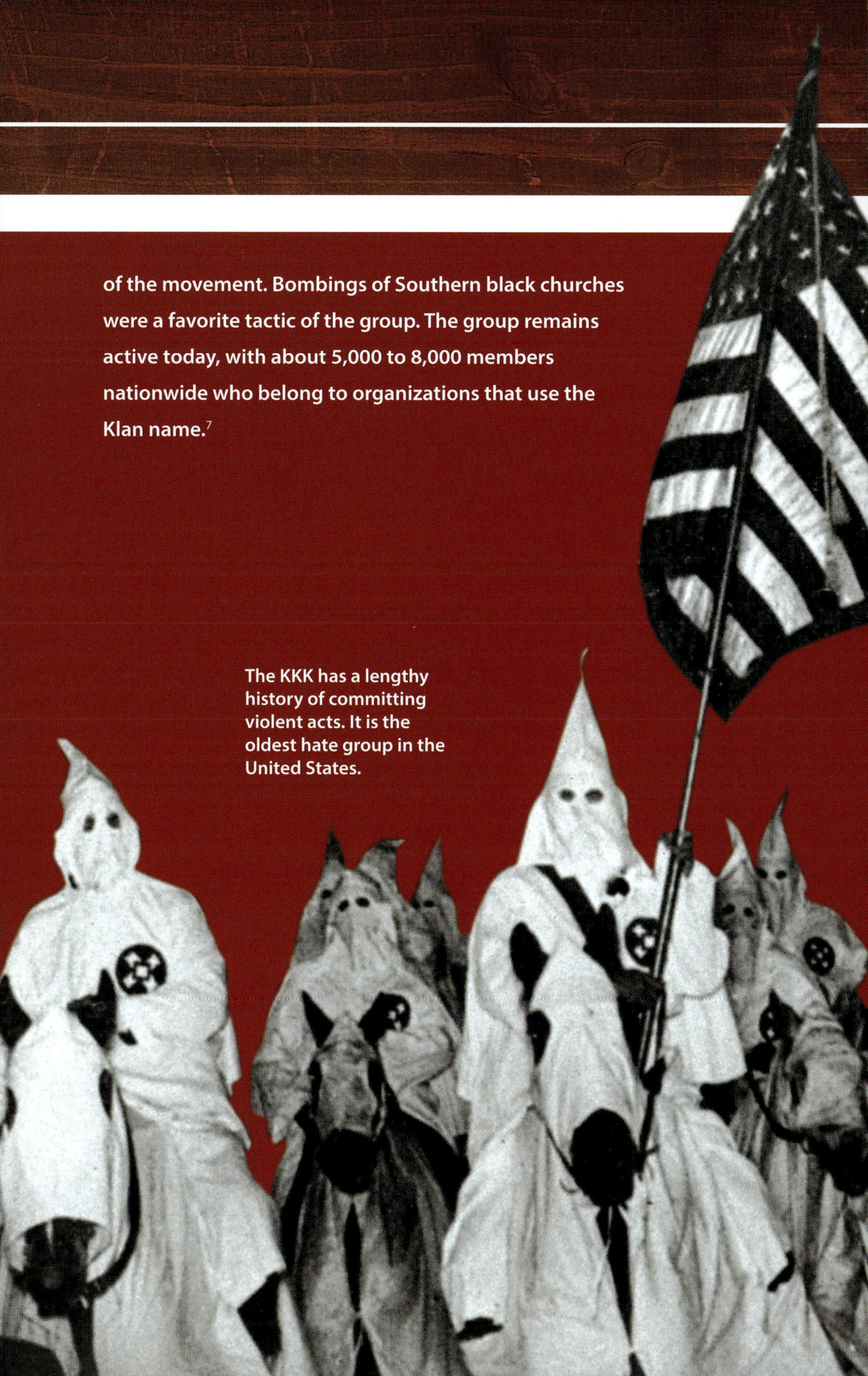

of the movement. Bombings of Southern black churches were a favorite tactic of the group. The group remains active today, with about 5,000 to 8,000 members nationwide who belong to organizations that use the Klan name.[7]

The KKK has a lengthy history of committing violent acts. It is the oldest hate group in the United States.

CHAPTER SEVEN

THE END OF RECONSTRUCTION

The United States was in trouble. White Southerners were resentful and humiliated by Radical Reconstruction. The KKK and other white supremacist terror groups threatened progress in the South. By the fall of 1876, eight of the 11 formerly seceded states were controlled by redeemers—Southern Democrats who wanted to redeem their states from Radical control and return blacks to their prewar status of second-class citizens.

THE DISPUTED ELECTION

The Republicans nominated Governor Rutherford B. Hayes of Ohio as their 1876 presidential candidate. Hayes was a moderate Republican. The Democrats nominated Samuel Tilden, the governor

Rutherford B. Hayes was a veteran of the Civil War.

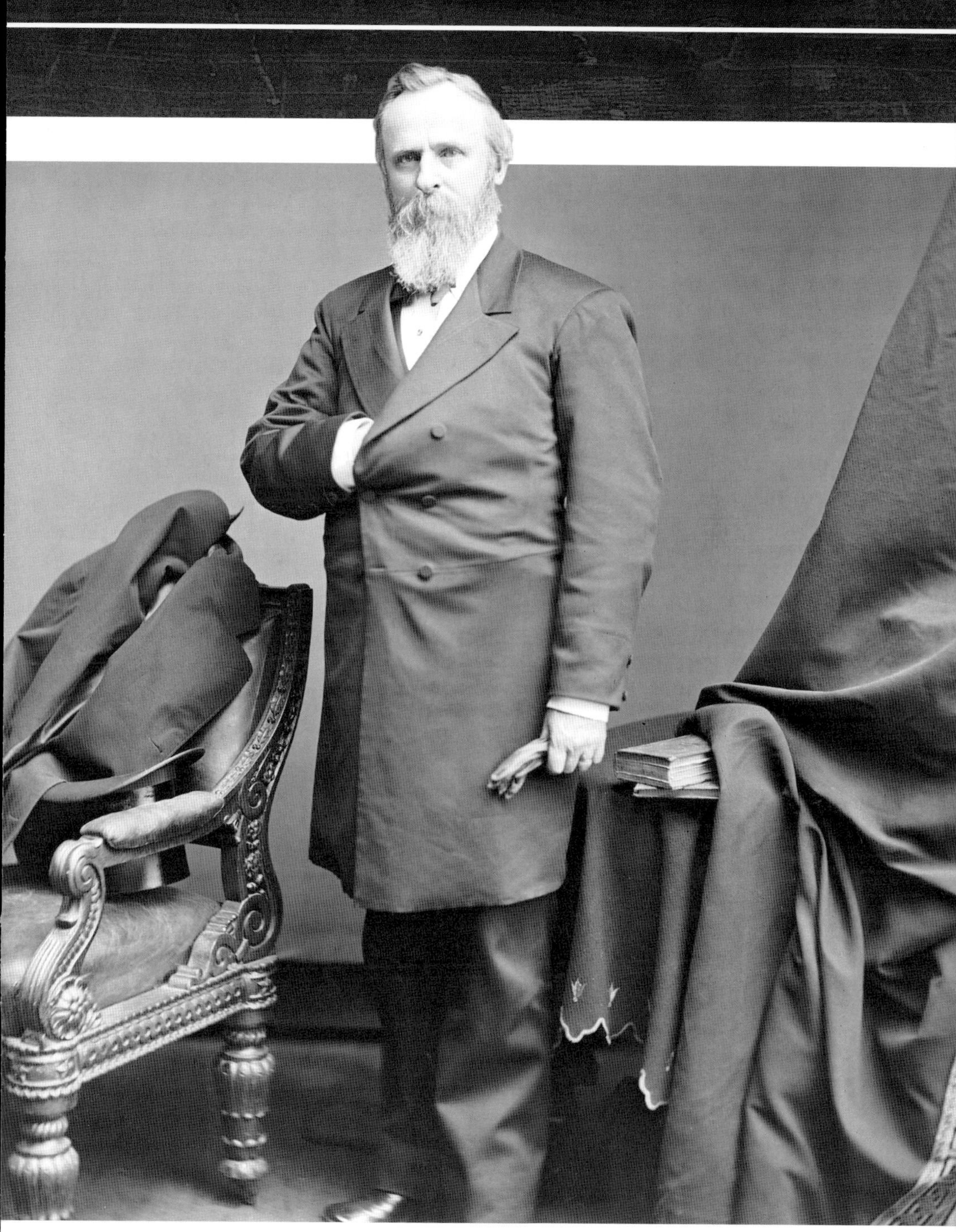

of New York. Many liberal, non-Radical Republicans supported Tilden. "It was quite clear that, whoever emerged victorious, Reconstruction was doomed," writes Foner.[1]

When the votes were counted, Tilden led in the electoral vote count, 184 to 165.[2] He needed only one more electoral vote to win the election. However, some electoral votes were in dispute in the three Southern states still held by the Republicans—Florida, Louisiana, and South Carolina. Congress appointed a commission to sort out the dispute and declare a winner.

A deal was struck. In the so-called Compromise of 1877, the Democrats agreed to accept a Hayes victory and to respect the voting and civil rights of African Americans, provided Hayes agreed to several conditions. Hayes would have to withdraw all federal troops from the South and recognize Democratic control of the region. Hayes would also have to place a prominent Southern politician on his cabinet and provide government aid to the Texas and Pacific Railway. On March 2, 1877, the commission awarded all the disputed electoral votes to Hayes, making him the nineteenth president of the United States.

RECONSTRUCTION DOOMED

In April, Hayes ordered federal troops out of Louisiana and South Carolina. By this time, Florida had already chosen a Democratic governor, and the troops had departed. The only protection for the freedmen's civil rights was gone. The Democrats now controlled every state in the South, and Reconstruction was dead. The era in which African Americans won elections to government offices and the federal government protected them was over.

Unlike Johnson, who publicly expressed antiblack views, Hayes supported African American rights. He had opposed slavery and its extension into western territories. As the governor of Ohio, he fought for voting rights for African Americans and was his state's leading crusader for the ratification of the Fourteenth Amendment. From the earliest days of his campaign for the presidency, Hayes affirmed his support of blacks' rights. "What the South most needs is peace. . . . There can be no enduring peace, if the constitutional rights of any portion of the people are habitually disregarded," Hayes said when accepting his party's nomination.[4]

Hayes believed the assurances he received from Southern Democratic political leaders who claimed they would protect blacks' rights. But in practice, Democrats failed to honor their word. To suppress the black vote, Democrats took control of local voter registration boards. Positions that black people had been elected to were changed to appointed positions, and white people replaced blacks.

WHAT DID IT MEAN?

The South's so-called redeemers set a course of undoing Reconstruction by limiting the political power of black people and limiting their opportunities

In 2018, some African Americans still had trouble voting in elections.

for economic and social advancement. Public education—
one of the finest achievements of Reconstruction—
was hit hardest. For example, Mississippi and Alabama
eliminated school taxes, forcing local communities to
support the system. Black schools suffered the most,
and the gap between spending for black and white
students skyrocketed. Southern schools remained racially
segregated, and white schools received more public
money. Fewer black schools existed, and most had poorer
facilities and fewer supplies and qualified teachers than
white schools.

The lack of Southern school spending in the
post-Reconstruction era extends into the present day. In
2016, each state spent an average of $11,762 on public

education per student. However, that year, the average amount spent by Southern states that had seceded in 1861 was $9,635 per student.[5]

Redeemers seized control of local and state politics by limiting the influence of black voters. Voting districts were rearranged to reduce black and Republican voting power. States introduced poll taxes and literacy tests to restrict African American voting—tactics that remained in use well into the 1900s. The voting restrictions also had the potential to prevent many white people from voting. However, shrewd redeemers found a way around the taxes and tests by enacting a grandfather clause. This law essentially provided exemptions to white men.

Criminal laws were instituted specifically to single out black people. Penalties for small crimes, such as burglary and theft of livestock, were increased. As in the days of the Black Codes, people could be arrested for being unemployed or leaving one employer for another. Enforcement of the laws was unfair and discriminatory, as black people were targeted more frequently. In some states, convicts were hired out to work for mining and railroad companies as forced labor. The vast majority of the men were African Americans jailed for small crimes.

Redeemers also sought to keep black people at the bottom of the Southern economy. This was largely accomplished by controlling the black labor force. Formerly enslaved people needed jobs. Southern planters needed workers. During Reconstruction, a system called sharecropping developed in which the landlord, most often white, allowed a tenant to work the land in exchange for a share of the crop. Tenants typically signed a one-year contract or lease to use the land. Landlords often provided the tenant with equipment, food, and seed, which the tenant would pay for at the end of the growing season.

Many sharecroppers fell into deep debt, owing more to the landlord than they were able to repay. Poor harvests

The sharecropping system was a way to keep black people in inferior positions compared with whites.

and high taxes on nearly everything the sharecropper owned—such as tools and farm animals—could leave the tenant with nothing at year's end. Sharecroppers often wound up in a vicious circle of debt, ultimately working the landlord's land for nothing—as enslaved people had done in pre–Civil War years.

Combined with other redeemer actions—tax cuts and reduced state budget and services—the agricultural South "sank even further into poverty," writes Foner, though "black farmers in the post-Reconstruction decades suffered the most from the region's overall condition."[6]

The "redemption" of the South repressed the emergence of African Americans as a political and social force in the region. Most black people were angered or frustrated by the dramatic turn of events. "We obey laws; others make them," wrote Charles Harris, a veteran Union army soldier and former representative in the Alabama legislature. "We support state educational institutions, whose doors are virtually closed against us. . . . From these and many other oppressions . . . our people long to be *free*."[7]

CHAPTER EIGHT

THE MODERN ERA

Reconstruction was an era marked by numerous achievements and several notable failures. Slavery was ended forever in the United States, and the Thirteenth, Fourteenth, and Fifteenth Amendments were added to the Constitution. On paper, African Americans gained civil rights, including the right to vote for men. The economy and infrastructure of the South was rebuilt. State-funded public institutions were launched. And the seceded South reunited with the Union.

On the other hand, Reconstruction failed to protect the gains made by freedmen. Black people continued to suffer from persecution and discrimination. Despite emancipation, many black

During the civil rights movement, people fought for the same treatment for white and black people.

WE DEMAND INTEGRATED SCHOOLS NOW!
WE DEMAND DECENT HOUSING NOW!
I.U.E. AFL-CIO FOR FULL EMPLOYMENT
UAW SAYS in FREEDOM WE ARE BORN- IN FREEDOM WE MUST LIVE
I.U.E. FIRST BAPTIST CHURCH
UAW SAYS END SEGREGATED RULES IN PUBLIC SCHOOLS
WE MARCH FOR INTEGRATED SCHOOLS NOW!
WE DEMAND VOTING RIGHTS NOW!
WE MARCH FOR JOBS FOR ALL NOW!
WE DEMAND VOTING RIGHTS NOW! END SEGREGATED RULES IN PUBLIC SCHOOLS
WE MARCH FOR JOBS FOR ALL NOW!
NO U.S. DOUGH TO HELP JIM CROW GROW
WE DEMAND AN END TO POLICE BRUTALITY NOW!
MARCH FOR JOBS FOR NOW
WE MARCH FOR EFFECTIVE CIVIL RIGHTS LAWS NOW

people remained poor and undereducated. The practice of sharecropping forced black people to rely on whites. In the end, control of the South remained in the hands of whites who held deep-seated prejudices against black people.

The Jim Crow days of legalized discrimination that marked the post-Reconstruction era lasted nearly 100 years. The failings of Reconstruction gave rise to a renewed fight for equality, which some historians have called the Second Reconstruction. Important events in the fight for equal rights began during the 1940s. In 1947, Jackie Robinson became the first African American in the modern era to play in Major League Baseball. In October 1947, President Harry S. Truman called for anti-lynching laws and the end to poll taxes. Months later, on July 26, 1948, Truman issued an executive order abolishing segregation in the US armed forces.

SCHOOL INTEGRATION AND MORE

Integrating public schools received a boost in the 1954 Supreme Court case *Brown v. Board of Education*. Overturning its verdict in an 1896 case, *Plessy v. Ferguson*, the Supreme Court ruled that segregation of public schools was unconstitutional. "Segregation of white and colored children in public schools has a detrimental effect upon the colored children," declared Chief Justice Earl Warren. "In the field of public education, the doctrine of 'separate but equal' has no place. Separate educational facilities are inherently unequal."[1]

Many Southern states openly defied the court's decision. In some parts of the South, whites closed down local school systems or used state funds to create white-only private schools. Responding to the outright defiance in 1957, President Dwight D. Eisenhower was forced to dispatch army soldiers to Little Rock, Arkansas, to ensure black students were admitted to a high school. Three years later, federal marshals had to escort a young black student past an angry mob of whites so she could attend her first day of class in an all-white elementary school in New Orleans.

But desegregation didn't stop there. In 1955 to 1956, there was a boycott of the Montgomery, Alabama, bus system by blacks and supportive whites. This resulted in the Supreme Court–ordered desegregation of the city's public transportation.

THE BARRIERS FALL

Despite many acts of violence against black rights activists, the civil rights movement in the mid-1900s gained momentum and began to win groundbreaking legislation. On July 2, 1964, President Lyndon B. Johnson signed the Civil Rights Act of 1964. The new law prohibited discrimination on the basis of race, color, religion, sex, or national origin in public places, provided for the integration of schools and other public facilities, and outlawed employment discrimination. The landmark legislation dealt the death blow to legalized segregation in the South.

African American voting rights gained protection with the Voting Rights Act of 1965, which outlawed the literacy tests and poll taxes used by many Southern states to suppress the black vote. As a result of the measure, African American voter registration increased in the South. The creation of districts with a majority of black voters helped more African Americans gain seats in Congress.

The final major piece of civil rights legislation was the Civil Rights Act of 1968. Also known as the Fair Housing Act, the law prohibited discrimination in the

President Johnson pressured Congress to pass the 1968 Civil Rights Act. Johnson signed it into law in April 1968.

sale and rental of housing. On April 11, 1968, Congress passed the act—seven days after the assassination of civil rights leader Dr. Martin Luther King Jr., one of the law's strongest supporters.

The Racial Divide

Despite the efforts of Reconstruction and the civil rights movement, African Americans remained on unequal footing compared with white people. Today, large gaps continue to exist between blacks and whites in major areas of daily life, including wealth, education and academic achievement, housing, employment, and health care.

Wealth—an individual's or family's total financial worth—allows families to live in better neighborhoods, pay for their children's education, and enjoy a happier, healthier lifestyle. A large gap exists in wealth between white and black households in the United States. In 2016, African Americans held roughly one-tenth the wealth of white Americans.[2] In addition, black people are less likely to own homes than whites. Discrimination and segregation in the job market also causes African Americans to have fewer opportunities for stable jobs, decent wages, and retirement benefits at work.

The scarcity of well-paying jobs for African Americans contributes to the enormous gap in poverty between black and white people. In 2016, roughly 9 percent of white Americans lived in poverty, compared with 22 percent of blacks who were below the poverty line.[3]

African Americans tend to start new businesses less frequently than whites, and when they do, the businesses perform more poorly than white-owned businesses.

Black businesses have lower sales and profits and hire fewer employees. African American businesses also have higher closure rates than white-owned firms. Among the reasons for the high failure rate of black-owned businesses are lack of experience and insufficient funding.

EDUCATION ACHIEVEMENT

In 2017, the US Department of Education released a study conducted by the National Center for Education Statistics comparing trends of racial and ethnic groups. The report showed that from 1992 through 2015, the average reading and math scores for white fourth, eighth, and twelfth graders in both public and private schools were higher than those of their black peers. Other studies indicate similar gaps between white and black academic achievement.

The inequity between wealthier and poorer districts may explain the gap in education achievement. Most public school districts in the United States are funded by local property taxes. Higher-income towns and school districts—often mainly white—can afford new textbooks and computers, as well as guidance counselors and school psychologists. Lower-income areas populated by minority groups collect fewer taxes and therefore have fewer dollars to spend on education.

A significant gap in achievement is also seen in higher education. Roughly 36.2 percent of white students compared with 22.5 percent of black students complete four years of college.[4] Studies have consistently demonstrated that college-educated individuals earn more money than nongraduates. In 2018, the US Bureau of Labor Statistics reported that people with a bachelor's degree earn $461 more per week than those with a high school diploma and no college. Employees with a master's degree earn nearly twice as much per week as those with no college learning.[5]

HEALTH CARE

African Americans also have worse access to health care and a poorer quality of care than white people in the United States. The gap between the races is significant in several important areas of health and health care. White women get screened for breast cancer at higher rates than African American women. And black patients are less likely to be tested for high cholesterol—a major cause of heart disease and stroke—than whites.

The overall poorer state of health care for African Americans has its roots in the Black Codes and Jim Crow laws. Hospitals and doctor's offices were strictly segregated by race. Education segregation and the inadequate number of schools and colleges led to fewer trained black medical professionals being available to work in predominantly black communities. Hospitals and clinics

In 2019, the achievement gap still existed between black and white students.

in such geographically segregated areas were understaffed and underfunded—conditions that still exist in many facilities throughout the country.

The prospects for improved health care in some states, for blacks and whites both, are not bright. As of December 2018, eight of the 11 states that practiced slavery and seceded from the Union had decided not to expand Medicaid benefits to their residents. Medicaid is a federal program that provides health coverage for some low-income people, the elderly, and people with disabilities.

The Justice System

Racial disparities exist in the US justice system as well—
as they did in the later years of Reconstruction under
redeemer legislatures. Today, African Americans are jailed
in state prisons five times more frequently than whites.
In some states, the rate is ten times more.[6] In 2016, black
people made up 12 percent of the US adult population yet
accounted for 33 percent of the prison population. White
people accounted for 64 percent of the nation's population
but 30 percent of prisoners.[7]

The mass jailing of black people is the subject of
filmmaker Ava DuVernay's *13th*, a 2016 documentary
that explores racism in the US justice system. The title of
the film comes from the Thirteenth Amendment, which
abolished slavery with the exception of punishment for
a crime. DuVernay believes that antiblack sentiments are
the major cause of the disproportionate jailing of blacks.
"We now have more African Americans under criminal
supervision than all the slaves back in the 1850s," declared
US senator Cory Booker in the movie's trailer.[8]

Harsh drug laws enacted in the 1990s are one of the
factors for the racial disparity. Though blacks and whites
use and sell drugs at roughly the same rate, black people
are more likely than whites to be arrested for drug-related
crimes overall. Another possible explanation for the gap is

Controversial Symbols of the Past

Many white Southerners claim the Confederate battle flag is an emblem of Southern heritage and a memorial to their ancestors who fought and died in the Civil War. In 1962, the flag was flown above the capitol dome of South Carolina and remained there until 2015. To others, the flag is a symbol of hate, racism, and oppression. The Confederate flag has become a controversial symbol for many Americans, and many people oppose its display in public places. A poll conducted in 2015 indicated that 75 percent of Southern whites viewed the flag as a symbol of regional pride, while 72 percent of African Americans consider the flag a symbol of racism.[9]

Monuments honoring Confederate soldiers and political leaders are also hotly contested symbols of the South's past. Many Americans, including Southern whites, are demanding their towns remove the monuments. Several Southern states have laws prohibiting local governments from removing them. But in some cities, people have torn down the monuments. Many people who object to the monuments claim most of the statues were erected during the Jim Crow era and during the civil rights movement as a means of asserting white supremacy.

the suspect's initial contact with law enforcement officers. Police throughout the country often use a technique called racial profiling to identify would-be suspects. Racial profiling occurs when law enforcement agents target individuals for stops, searches, and arrests based on their race, ethnicity, or religion. Racial profiling is illegal and violates the Constitution.

Traffic stops are the most common form of racial
profiling. Studies have consistently shown that African
Americans are more likely to be stopped by police in their
vehicles than whites. Targets of racial profiling are likely to
be asked whether they are carrying weapons or drugs and
asked to leave their vehicles. Some people are searched or
have their vehicles searched.

Defenders of racial profiling argue that the technique
is part of sound investigative practices. Opponents of the
practice claim that profiling is nothing but discrimination
that targets African Americans because of racist impulses.

The patterns and events of the Reconstruction era still echo today. Huge gaps in education, employment, and wealth are present between white people and people of color. Segregation exists in schools, housing, and other institutions. Gross inequalities between the races exist in the nation's justice and health-care systems. Much work remains to be done to achieve equality and remedy the legacy of Reconstruction's failings. The responsibility for fixing the problem lies with all Americans.

DISCUSSION STARTERS

- What instances of racism and discrimination do you see today?

- How do you think academic achievement in school affects people later in their lives?

- Do you think growing up in poverty hurts a person's chance of becoming financially stable? Explain your answer.

1861

The Civil War begins.

1863

On January 1, Lincoln's Emancipation Proclamation goes into effect; on December 8, Lincoln announces his Ten Percent Plan, the first official plan for postwar Reconstruction.

1864

In July, Congress passes the Wade-Davis Bill, its own plan for Reconstruction; Lincoln vetoes the bill.

1865

Lincoln is assassinated by John Wilkes Booth and Vice President Andrew Johnson assumes the presidency; the Civil War ends; state legislatures in the South begin passing Black Codes to limit the rights of former slaves; the Thirteenth Amendment receives congressional approval.

1866

Congress passes the Civil Rights Bill, giving all people born in the United States citizenship.

1867

On March 2, Congress begins passing the Military Reconstruction Acts over Johnson's veto.

1868

On February 24, the House of Representatives votes to impeach President Johnson; in May the Senate fails to vote for impeachment; the Fourteenth Amendment is ratified; in November, General Ulysses S. Grant is elected president of the United States.

1870

The Fifteenth Amendment
is ratified, giving African
American men the right to vote;
Congress passes the first of
two Enforcement Acts to halt
antiblack violence by radical
terrorist groups; by July all of the
former Confederate states are
readmitted to the Union.

1873

The Supreme Court rules in the
Slaughterhouse Cases, limiting
the Fourteenth Amendment.

1876

The Supreme Court ruling in
United States v. Cruikshank
further limits the scope of the
Fourteenth Amendment.

1877

Republican Rutherford B.
Hayes becomes president and
promises to withdraw all federal
troops from the South; the era
of Reconstruction ends.

1954

In *Brown v. Board of Education*,
the Supreme Court declares
that public school segregation
is unconstitutional.

1964

President Lyndon B. Johnson
signs the Civil Rights Act
of 1964.

1968

Congress passes the Civil Rights
Act of 1968.

SIGNIFICANT EVENTS

- Abraham Lincoln issued the Emancipation Proclamation in 1863, freeing some enslaved people in Confederate states. That same year, Lincoln began his plan for Reconstruction.

- Confederate general Robert E. Lee surrendered to the Union on April 9, 1865. Approximately 620,000 Americans died in the Civil War.

- The Ku Klux Klan was established in 1865.

- The Fourteenth Amendment was added to the Constitution in 1868.

- In 1868, the House of Representatives voted to impeach President Andrew Johnson.

- Rutherford B. Hayes became president in 1877 and withdrew federal troops that were in the South. Reconstruction ended.

KEY PLAYERS

- Lincoln issued the first federal policy of Reconstruction in 1863. Some people saw Lincoln's Ten Percent Plan as a lenient and charitable program of reunification.

- Johnson succeeded Lincoln as president in April 1865, following Lincoln's assassination. Johnson proposed his own plan for Reconstruction that year.

- Radical Republicans believed Congress, not the president, had the authority to formulate Reconstruction policies. Radicals supported black rights, land confiscation, and stern terms for seceded states to be readmitted to the Union. Radicals sharply opposed the Southern governments established under Johnson's Reconstruction plan.

IMPACT ON SOCIETY

Most historians regard Reconstruction as a failure, though its
legacy left behind both positive and negative effects. Through
Reconstruction, African Americans gained many political and
civil freedoms through constitutional amendments—including
the right for men to vote. Republican-led Southern governments
established public school systems for black and white people
during Reconstruction and helped rebuild the South's devastated
infrastructure. On the negative side, violent white supremacy
groups, such as the Ku Klux Klan, were founded during
Reconstruction. Antiblack violence and racist laws and practices
are also part of Reconstruction's legacy, lasting well into the
present day.

QUOTE

"What the South most needs is peace. . . . There can be no enduring
peace, if the constitutional rights of any portion of the people are
habitually disregarded."

—President Rutherford B. Hayes, 1876

abolition
The act of officially banning something.

amnesty
An official pardon granted to people who have been convicted of political offenses or crimes.

bondage
The state of being under the control of someone when it is against one's will.

denounce
To condemn.

disparity
A great difference between two or more things.

impeach
To charge an elected official with wrongdoing.

inflation
An increase in the price of goods and services.

infrastructure

The physical structures, such as roads, railways, and power plants, that make it possible for a city or nation to function.

Jim Crow laws

State and local laws passed in the 1880s in the South to racially segregate black people.

militia

A military force made up of nonprofessional fighters.

secede

To formally withdraw from a political union.

segregation

The practice of separating groups of people based on race, gender, ethnicity, or other factors.

suffrage

The right to vote in a political election.

veto

The power of a president to reject a bill passed by the legislative branch.

white supremacy

The belief that white people are superior to all other races.

SELECTED BIBLIOGRAPHY

Foner, Eric. *Forever Free: The Story of Emancipation and Reconstruction.* Knopf, 2005.

Franklin, John Hope. *Reconstruction after the Civil War.* U of Chicago P, 2013.

Perman, Michael. *Emancipation and Reconstruction.* Harlan Davidson, 2003.

FURTHER READINGS

Cummings, Judy Dodge. *The Emancipation Proclamation.* Abdo, 2017.

Hamen, Susan E. *Civil War Aftermath and Reconstruction.* Abdo, 2017.

ONLINE RESOURCES

To learn more about reconstructing the South, please visit **abdobooklinks.com** or scan this QR code. These links are routinely monitored and updated to provide the most current information available.

MORE INFORMATION

For more information on this subject, contact or visit the
following organizations:

NATIONAL CIVIL RIGHTS MUSEUM

450 Mulberry St.
Memphis, TN 38103
901-521-9699

civilrightsmuseum.org

The National Civil Rights Museum has information on the history of
slavery in the United States, the Civil War, Reconstruction, and the civil
rights movement.

NATIONAL MUSEUM OF AFRICAN AMERICAN HISTORY & CULTURE

1400 Constitution Ave. NW
Washington, DC 20560
844-750-3012

nmaahc.si.edu

The National Museum of African American History & Culture opened
in 2016. This museum has tens of thousands of artifacts illuminating
African American history and culture. There are also exhibits on the
history of slavery.

CHAPTER 1. AN UNPRECEDENTED CHALLENGE

1. "Confederate States of America—Declaration of the Immediate Causes Which Induce and Justify the Secession of South Carolina from the Federal Union." *Yale Law School*, n.d., web.archive.org. Accessed 10 Jan. 2019.

2. "The Declaration of Causes of Seceding States." *American Battlefield Trust*, n.d., battlefields.org. Accessed 10 Jan. 2019.

3. James Oliver Horton. "Confronting Slavery and Revealing the 'Lost Cause.'" *National Park Service*, n.d., nps.gov. Accessed 10 Jan. 2019.

4. "'Corner Stone' Speech." *Teaching American History*, n.d., teachingamericanhistory.org. Accessed 10 Jan. 2019.

5. "Newspaper Account of a Meeting between Black Religious Leaders and Union Military Authorities." *Freedmen & Southern Society Project*, n.d., freedmen.umd.edu. Accessed 10 Jan. 2019.

6. "The Cost of War: Killed, Wounded, Captured, and Missing." *American Battlefield Trust*, n.d., battlefields.org. Accessed 10 Jan. 2019.

7. "Reconstruction." *History*, 29 Oct. 2009, history.com. Accessed 10 Jan. 2019.

8. Roger L. Ransom. "The Economies of the Civil War." *Economic History*, n.d., eh.net. Accessed 10 Jan. 2019.

9. Eric Foner. *Forever Free: The Story of Emancipation and Reconstruction.* Knopf, 2005. 14.

CHAPTER 2. THE STATE OF A NATION

1. Dr. Gayle Olson-Raymer. "The Civil War: Goals, Strategies, and Consequences." *Humboldt State University*, n.d., users.humboldt.edu. Accessed 10 Jan. 2019.

2. Benjamin T. Arrington. "Industry and Economy during the Civil War." *National Park Service*, n.d., nps.gov. Accessed 10 Jan. 2019.

3. Carl Schurz. "Report on the Condition of the South." *W. W. Norton*, 1865, wwnorton.com. Accessed 10 Jan. 2019.

4. Harvey Wish, ed. *Reconstruction in the South, 1865–1877: First-Hand Accounts of the American Southland after the Civil War, by Northerners & Southerners.* Farrar, Straus and Giroux, 1965. 7.

5. Eric Foner. *A Short History of Reconstruction, 1863–1877.* Harper, 2015.

CHAPTER 3. PRESIDENTIAL RECONSTRUCTION

1. "The Emancipation Proclamation 1863." *American History*, n.d., let.rug.nl. Accessed 10 Jan. 2019.

2. David Herbert Donald. *The Civil War and Reconstruction*. Norton, 2001. 512.

3. John Hope Franklin. *Reconstruction after the Civil War*. U of Chicago P, 2013. 27–28.

4. Franklin, *Reconstruction after the Civil War*, 28.

5. "Andrew Johnson." *Understanding Prejudice*, n.d., secure.understandingprejudice.org. Accessed 10 Jan. 2019.

6. Donald, *The Civil War and Reconstruction*, 526.

7. "Address of the Colored State Convention to the People of the State of South Carolina." *History Matters*, n.d., historymatters.gmu.edu. Accessed 10 Jan. 2019.

8. Eric Foner. *Reconstruction: America's Unfinished Revolution, 1863–1877*. Perennial Classics, 2002. 203.

CHAPTER 4. CONGRESS PUSHES BACK

1. "The Civil War: The Senate's Story." *United States Senate*, n.d., senate.gov. Accessed 10 Jan. 2019.

2. John Hope Franklin. *Reconstruction after the Civil War*. U of Chicago P, 2013. 58.

3. *Report of the Joint Committee on Reconstruction, at the First Session, Thirty-Ninth Congress*. US Government Printing Office, 1866. 55.

4. *Report of the Joint Committee on Reconstruction*, xx.

5. "Veto of the Civil Rights Bill." *Teaching American History*, 27 Mar. 1866, teachingamericanhistory.org. Accessed 10 Jan. 2019.

6. "Memphis Riot, 1866." *Black Past*, n.d., blackpast.org. Accessed 10 Jan. 2019.

7. Philip H. Sheridan. *Personal Memoirs of P. H. Sheridan, Volume 2*. Digital Scanning. 236.

8. *United States Congressional Serial Set, Volume 1292*. US Government Printing Office, 1867. 11.

9. Peter Carlson. "Thaddeus Stevens." *History Net*, 19 Feb. 2013, historynet.com. Accessed 10 Jan. 2019.

CHAPTER 5. CONGRESSIONAL RECONSTRUCTION

1. "The Impeachment of Andrew Johnson (1868) President of the United States." *United States Senate*, n.d., senate.gov. Accessed 10 Jan. 2019.

2. "The Senate Votes on a Presidential Impeachment." *United States Senate*, n.d., senate.gov. Accessed 10 Jan. 2019.

3. "Black Leaders during Reconstruction." *History*, 24 June 2010, history.com. Accessed 10 Jan. 2019.

4. Jennifer Latson. "How the First Black US Senator Was Nearly Kept from His Seat." *Time*, 25 Feb. 2014, time.com. Accessed 10 Jan. 2019.

5. Eric Foner. *Reconstruction: America's Unfinished Revolution, 1863–1877.* Perennial Classics, 2002. 426.

6. "White Mob Kidnaps and Whips Black Georgia Legislator for Promoting Equal Rights." *Equal Justice Initiative*, n.d., racialinjustice.eji.org. Accessed 10 Jan. 2019.

7. Douglas R. Egerton. *The Wars of Reconstruction: The Brief, Violent History of America's Most Progressive Era.* Bloomsbury, 2013. 257.

8. Egerton, *The Wars of Reconstruction*, 259.

9. "Literacy from 1870 to 1979." *National Center for Education Statistics*, n.d., nces.ed.gov. Accessed 10 Jan. 2019.

CHAPTER 6. THE TIDE TURNS

1. Harvey Wish, ed. *Reconstruction in the South, 1865–1877: First-Hand Accounts of the American Southland after the Civil War, by Northerners & Southerners.* Farrar, Straus and Giroux, 1965. 165.

2. Allen W. Trelease. *White Terror: The Ku Klux Klan Conspiracy and Southern Reconstruction.* Harper & Row, 1971. xlvii.

3. Eric Foner. *Forever Free: The Story of Emancipation and Reconstruction.* Knopf, 2005. 194.

4. Didi Kuo. *Clientelism, Capitalism, and Democracy: The Rise of Programmatic Politics in the United States and Britain.* Cambridge UP, 2018.

5. "The Hamburg Massacre (1876)." *Black Past*, n.d., blackpast.org. Accessed 10 Jan. 2019.

6. Joshua Rothman. "When Bigotry Paraded through the Streets." *Atlantic*, 4 Dec. 2016, theatlantic.com. Accessed 10 Jan. 2019.

7. "Ku Klux Klan." *Southern Poverty Law Center*, n.d., splcenter.org. Accessed 10 Jan. 2019.

CHAPTER 7. THE END OF RECONSTRUCTION

1. Eric Foner. *Forever Free: The Story of Emancipation and Reconstruction.* Knopf, 2005. 197.

2. "United States Presidential Election of 1876." *Encyclopedia Britannica*, n.d., britannica.com. Accessed 10 Jan. 2019.

3. Harvey Wish, ed. *Reconstruction in the South, 1865–1877: First-Hand Accounts of the American Southland after the Civil War, by Northerners & Southerners.* Farrar, Straus and Giroux, 1965. 304–318.

4. "Hayes Accepts the Republican Party's Presidential Nomination." *Rutherford B. Hayes Presidential Library & Museums*, n.d., rbhayes.org. Accessed 10 Jan. 2019.

5. "Education Spending per Student by State." *Governing*, 1 June 2018, governing.com. Accessed 10 Jan. 2019.

6. Foner, *Forever Free*, 203.

7. Eric Foner. *Reconstruction: America's Unfinished Revolution, 1863–1877.* Perennial Classics, 2002. 601.

CHAPTER 8. THE MODERN ERA

1. "The Court's Decision." *Smithsonian*, n.d., americanhistory.si.edu. Accessed 10 Jan. 2019.

2. "Systematic Inequality." *Center for American Progress*, 21 Feb. 2018, americanprogress.org. Accessed 10 Jan. 2019.

3. Heather Long. "African Americans Are the Only US Racial Group Earning Less Than in 2000." *Chicago Tribune*, 15 Sept. 2017, chicagotribune.com. Accessed 10 Jan. 2019.

4. Mitchell Wellman. "Report: The Race Gap in Higher Education Is Very Real." *USA Today*, 7 Mar. 2017, usatoday.com. Accessed 10 Jan. 2019.

5. Elka Torpey. "Measuring the Value of Education." *Bureau of Labor Statistics*, Apr. 2018, bls.gov. Accessed 10 Jan. 2019.

6. Ashley Nellis. "The Color of Justice: Racial and Ethnic Disparity in State Prisons." *Sentencing Project*, 14 June 2016, sentencingproject.org. Accessed 10 Jan. 2019.

7. John Gramlich. "The Gap between the Number of Blacks and Whites in Prison Is Shrinking." *Pew Research Center*, 12 Jan. 2018, pewresearch.org. Accessed 10 Jan. 2019.

8. Shenequa Golding. "Ava DuVernay's '13th' Takes a Historical Look at the Link between Slavery and Mass Incarceration." *Vibe*, 4 Oct. 2016, vibe.com. Accessed 10 Jan. 2019.

9. Jennifer Agiesta. "Poll: Majority Sees Confederate Flag as Southern Pride Symbol, Not Racist." *CNN*, 2 July 2015, cnn.com. Accessed 10 Jan. 2019.

DUCHESS HARRIS, JD, PHD

Dr. Harris is a professor of American Studies at Macalester College and curator of the Duchess Harris Collection of ABDO books. She is also the coauthor of the titles in the collection, which features popular selections such as *Hidden Human Computers: The Black Women of NASA* and series including News Literacy and Being Female in America.

Before working with ABDO, Dr. Harris authored several other books on the topics of race, culture, and American history. She served as an associate editor for *Litigation News*, the American Bar Association Section of Litigation's quarterly flagship publication, and was the first editor in chief of *Law Raza*, an interactive online journal covering race and the law, published at William Mitchell College of Law. She has earned a PhD in American Studies from the University of Minnesota and a JD from William Mitchell College of Law.

NEL YOMTOV

Nel Yomtov is an award-winning author of nonfiction books and graphic novels for young readers. His writing passions include history, geography, the military, nature, sports, biographies, and careers. He has also written, edited, and colored hundreds of Marvel comic books. He has served as editorial director of a children's nonfiction book publisher and executive editor of Hammond World Atlas book division. Yomtov lives in the New York City area with his wife.